ESPECIALLY FOR

_____

FROM

D1565311

_____

DATE

_____

© 2011 by Barbour Publishing, Inc.

ISBN 978-1-61626-200-6

Compiled by Michael Ward in association with Snapdragon Group℠, Tulsa, OK.

Published by Barbour Publishing, Inc., P.O. Box 719, Uhrichsville, Ohio 44683, www.barbourbooks.com

Our mission is to publish and distribute inspirational products offering exceptional value and biblical encouragement to the masses.

Member of the
Evangelical Christian
Publishers Association

Printed in China.

Fun Facts for
FOOTBALL
FANS

BARBOUR
PUBLISHING

WHEN I PLAYED PRO FOOTBALL, I NEVER
SET OUT TO HURT ANYONE DELIBERATELY —
UNLESS IT WAS, YOU KNOW, IMPORTANT,
LIKE A LEAGUE GAME OR SOMETHING.

DICK BUTKUS

WHO HAS WON MORE SUPER BOWL MVP AWARDS?

A. Tom Brady (2)
B. Joe Montana (3)
C. Bart Starr (2)
D. Emmitt Smith (1)

With rugby at its roots, the first rules of American football were written in 1876. A touchdown was worth 4 points.

The official referee signal for a
first down is arm pointed toward
the defensive team's end zone. A first
down is attained when an offensive
team moves the ball 10 yards in
no more than 4 downs.

30 ◄40 50

The original National Football League was made up of three teams: The Pittsburgh Stars, the Philadelphia Athletics, and the Philadelphia Phillies. The two Philadelphia clubs were also professional baseball teams. The Athletics would later take residence in Oakland, sharing a stadium with football's Oakland Raiders.

IN 2010, HOW MANY NFL TEAMS HAD BIRD NAMES?

Answer: Five
(Seahawks, Falcons, Cardinals, Ravens, and Eagles)

Though considered by many to be the greatest quarterback to ever play the game, Joe Montana wasn't a first, or even a second round draft pick. It wasn't until the third round that the San Francisco 49ers made him the eighty-second overall pick.

CURLY LAMBEAU WAS NAMED
HEAD COACH OF THE GREEN BAY
PACKERS WHEN THE ORGANIZATION
BECAME A PUBLIC NONPROFIT
CORPORATION IN 1922.

30 ◄**40** **50**

The first NFL game held at night under lights
took place on November 3, 1929.
It featured the Providence Steam Roller
vs. the Chicago Cardinals.

THE REDSKINS MOVED TO
WASHINGTON IN 1937.
BEFORE THAT THEY WERE
THE BOSTON REDSKINS.

The Chicago Bears were named the Bears by George Halas, who chose a more rugged version of the already present Chicago Cubs.

The official referee signal for a personal foul is arms raised above the head, wrist striking wrist, followed by what the foul was for. For example, roughing the passer would result in the referee striking his wrists and raising his arm and swinging it forward.

#1

30 ◄40 50

Qualcomm Stadium, home of the San Diego Chargers, was originally called "Jack Murphy Stadium," named after the San Diego sportswriter who helped bring the Chargers from Los Angeles to San Diego.

The United States Football League (USFL) was formed in 1983. It lasted for only three seasons. Though able to sign the brightest stars college football had to offer, it couldn't generate enough revenue to offset the huge salary expenses it had taken on.

The Michigan Panthers won the first USFL Championship, defeating the Philadelphia Stars 24–22, despite the fact that the Stars had a better regular season record than the Panthers. The Stars went on to win the next two league championships.

Howard Cosell was well known as a commentator for Monday Night Football when the telecast first aired, and for his coverage of the Olympics and the boxing career of Mohammad Ali. What few know, though, is that he held a law degree from NYU.

30 ◄40 50

SOME PEOPLE THINK FOOTBALL IS A MATTER OF LIFE AND DEATH. I ASSURE YOU, IT'S MUCH MORE SERIOUS THAN THAT.

BILL SHANKLY

Glenn Scobey "Pop" Warner was one of the most accomplished coaches in college football history, coaching from 1895 to 1938. One of the original founders of youth football, his name is synonymous with junior tackle football throughout America.

KNUTE ROCKNE LED THE NOTRE DAME
FIGHTING IRISH OVER ARMY IN 1913,
HELPING ESTABLISH THE CATHOLIC
UNIVERSITY AS A FORCE TO BE
RECKONED WITH.

The official referee signal for a safety
is arms raised and palms together.
A safety is when an offensive player
is tackled in his own end zone
and is worth 2 points.

THE "FOUR HORSEMEN OF NOTRE DAME" WERE MADE UP OF HARRY STUHLDREHER, DON MILLER, JIM CROWLEY, AND ELMER LAYDEN, WHO PLAYED FOR THE IRISH DURING THE 1920S.

The Pac-10 College Football Conference was originally the PCC (Pacific Coast Conference). The charter members of the PCC were Cal, Washington, Oregon, and Oregon State. The PCC was disbanded in 1959.

The first Heisman trophy winner was Jay Berwanger, who won the award in 1935. Berwanger played halfback for the University of Chicago. He was the first player chosen in the 1936 NFL draft, the inaugural draft of the professional football league.

The name Buffalo Bills (other than the fact that they are located in Buffalo) refers to "Buffalo Bill" William F. Cody, a famous 1860s buffalo hunter who competed in a shooting match with Bill Comstock, the original Buffalo Bill. Cody won the match and exclusive right to use the name.

In 1970 there were 8 bowl games. By 2008, the number had grown to 34. While opponents of the growth feel the significance of playing in a bowl game has dwindled, proponents argue that it has paid substantial dividends to colleges throughout the country.

Keith Jackson, one of the greatest football commentators of all time, covered college football for fifty-four years. He popularized the term "Whoa, Nellie." Jackson is credited with nicknaming the Rose Bowl "The Grandaddy of Them All" and Michigan Stadium "The Big House."

Many consider the 1958 NFL Championship to be the greatest game ever played. The game featured the Baltimore Colts vs. the New York Giants at Yankee Stadium. In sudden death overtime, the Colts defeated the Giants 23–17.

FOOTBALL HELMETS BECAME
A MANDATORY PIECE OF
EQUIPMENT IN THE COLLEGE
GAME IN 1939. THE NFL ADOPTED
THE SAME PROVISION IN 1943.

#1

The Offensive Line is made up of five players:
the center, who snaps the ball to a back
(doesn't have to be the quarterback); two guards,
one to the left of the center and one to the right;
and two tackles lining up outside the guards.
It is the job of these individuals to protect the
quarterback and create an opening should one
of the backs choose to run the ball.

The Pittsburgh Steelers, founded in 1933, were originally called the Pittsburgh Pirates. They changed their name to the Steelers prior to the 1940 season.

HOW MANY YARDS DID ERIC DICKERSON RUSH FOR IN 1984?

A. 1,810
B. 1,573
C. 2,411
D. 2,105

◄ 10   ◄ 20

WIDE RECEIVERS PRIMARILY CATCH THE BALL, ALTHOUGH THEY ARE OFTEN REQUIRED TO BLOCK FOR A TEAMMATE RUNNING THE BALL, AND THEY WILL OCCASIONALLY THROW A PASS.

#1

Nobody has played more seasons than George Blanda. Blanda played twenty-six years with four different teams between 1949 and 1975: Chicago, Baltimore, Houston, and Oakland.

*Whatever your hand finds to do,
do with your might.*

ECCLESIASTES 9:10 NRSV

jackie slater and darrell green are the only two players to ever play 20 seasons with the same NFL team.

In the mid-1930s, The Associated Press (AP) began to solicit sports writers to determine who ranked as the top twenty college football teams in the nation.

30 ◂ 40 50

Len Dawson is the most accurate quarterback of all time, leading the league an astounding eight times in completion percentage.

WHEN THE DISCUSSION OF GREATEST QUARTERBACKS BEGINS, DAN MARINO'S NAME QUICKLY SURFACES. MARINO PASSED FOR MORE THAN 400 YARDS IN A GAME THIRTEEN TIMES.

The Cleveland Browns are named after Paul Brown, the team's first coach and general manager. The Browns left Cleveland and moved to Baltimore, where they became the Ravens. A few years later, Cleveland received a new franchise and once again named the team the Browns.

LaDainian Tomlinson holds the record for most points scored in a single season—186. Tomlinson set this record in 2006 when he rushed for 31 touchdowns.

30 ◄ 40 50

Al Michaels covered play-by-play for *Monday Night Football* for twenty years, joined by a variety of individuals throughout his tenure, including Dan Dierdorf and Frank Gifford. In 2002, John Madden joined Michaels in the *MNF* booth.

The dubious honor for most fumbles in a career goes to Warren Moon (161).
Moon also holds the record for most fumbles recovered (56).

WALTER CAMP IS CONSIDERED THE "FATHER OF AMERICAN FOOTBALL." A WRITER AND COACH, HE WAS A LEADING INNOVATOR FROM 1880 TO 1925.

FOOTBALL iSN'T A CONTACT SPORT,
iT'S A COLLiSiON SPORT.
DANCiNG iS A CONTACT SPORT.

DUFFY DAUGHERTY

30 ◂ 40 50

The Pittsburgh Steelers have won the most Super Bowl championships, winning four championships with Terry Bradshaw as the quarterback, and two championships with Ben Roethlisberger as the quarterback.

Many consider Adam Vinatieri
to be the greatest field goal kicker
of all time, though his name rarely
appears in the record books.
So why the best? Clutch. Vinatieri
kicked the deciding field goal
in three New England Patriot
Super Bowl wins.

The Dallas Cowboys were almost called the Dallas Rangers, as the Texas Rangers did not move from Washington DC (where they were the Senators) until 1972, twelve years after the Cowboys joined the NFL. There was, however, a local minor league team called the Rangers.

TIP:

Holding and throwing a football: all five fingers on the ball held as close to the end of the football as possible with at least the ring finger between the laces; ball ear high; release with the fingers out.

WHO ARE THE FASTEST MEN EVER TO PLAY IN THE NFL?

These five would make most lists:
Bob Hayes, Darrell Green, Cliff Branch,
Mel Gray, and Randy Moss.

BRETT FAVRE HAS THROWN
MORE INTERCEPTIONS THAN
ANY OTHER QUARTERBACK
IN NFL HISTORY. OF COURSE
HE HAS THROWN THE MOST
TOUCHDOWNS, TOO.

The first Super Bowl was played in 1967. It was played in the Los Angeles Coliseum and featured the Green Bay Packers vs. the Kansas City Chiefs. The Packers won the game 35–10.

Todd Dempsey and Jason Elam share the record for longest field goal—63 yards. Dempsey accomplished the feat in 1970; Elam in 1998.

30 ◂ 40 50

BERNIE KOSAR HOLDS THE RECORD FOR
MOST CONSECUTIVE PASSES THROWN
WITHOUT AN INTERCEPTION (308)
ACCOMPLISHED FROM 1990 TO 1991.

The New York Jets' team name was chosen based on two aspects. It sounded like "Mets" (the New York baseball team) and it was in close proximity to LaGuardia Airport.

THE PITTSBURGH STEELERS ARE THE ONLY TEAM TO DRAFT FOUR FUTURE HALL OF FAMERS IN THE SAME SEASON, DRAFTING LYNN SWANN, JACK LAMBERT, JOHN STALLWORTH, AND MIKE WEBSTER IN 1974.

The Dallas Cowboys have won 5 Super Bowl Championships—their first in 1971 (Super Bowl VI) and their last in 1995 (Super Bowl XXX).

#1

30 ◄40 50

TOM BRADY HOLDS THE RECORD
FOR MOST TOUCHDOWN PASSES
THROWN IN A SINGLE QUARTER (5),
ACCOMPLISHED ON OCTOBER 18, 2009.

The record for most rushing touchdowns in a single game is 6, accomplished by Ernie Nevers of the Chicago Cardinals in 1929. Nevers also pitched for the St. Louis Browns.

THE DALLAS COWBOYS ARE THE HIGHEST VALUED FRANCHISE IN AMERICAN SPORTS. VALUED AT OVER $1.6 BILLION, THEY EDGE OUT THE WASHINGTON REDSKINS, WHO ARE VALUED AT $1.5 BILLION.

Undoubtedly the greatest player
in Chicago Bears history is Walter
Payton. Nicknamed "Sweetness,"
he died from a rare liver cancer
at the young age of forty-five.

30 ◂ **40** **50**

THE RECORD FOR MOST CONSECUTIVE
FIELD GOALS MADE WAS SET BY
MIKE VANDERJAGT, WHO MADE 42
IN A ROW FROM 2002 TO 2004.

The Chicago Bears' rivalry with the Green Bay Packers dates back to 1921 and is one of the fiercest in all of sports, right up there with the Lakers/Celtics (NBA), Canadians/Bruins (NHL), and Yankees/Red Sox (MLB).

The official referee signal for a false start (offense drawing the defense across the line of scrimmage before the ball is snapped) is rolling the forearms over each other. Results in a 5-yard penalty against the offense.

All those who compete in the games use self-control so they can win a crown. That crown is an earthly thing that lasts only a short time, but our crown will never be destroyed. So I do not run without a goal. I fight like a boxer who is hitting something— not just the air.

1 CORINTHIANS 9:25–26 NCV

30   ◂ 40   50

THE RECORD FOR THE MOST RUSHING
YARDS IN A SINGLE GAME WAS SET BY
ADRIAN PETERSON ON NOVEMBER 4, 2007,
WHEN HE RAN FOR 296 YARDS.

The San Francisco 49ers won 5 Super Bowl championships over a fourteen-year period. Four of the championships were with Joe Montana guiding the team; the fifth was with Steve Young at the helm.

Kurt Warner, known as a great quarterback and even better man, played college football at little known Northern Iowa and did not become a starter until his senior season.

Sixteen Heisman winners, from 1935 to 2009, went on to become number one NFL draft picks. Only three, Paul Hornung, O. J. Simpson, and Earl Campbell went on to have Hall of Fame careers in the NFL.

BRETT FAVRE IS THE ONLY NFL PLAYER TO WIN THE AP NFL MVP. HE WON THE AWARD IN 1995, 1996, AND 1997.

BART STARR WAS THE
FIRST SUPER BOWL MVP.
HE COMPLETED 16 PASSES,
THROWING FOR 250 YARDS
WITH 2 TOUCHDOWNS AND
1 INTERCEPTION.

The official referee signal for pass interference (offensive and defensive) is arms extended forward, palms out.

Brett Favre's football career almost ended before it ever began. Not only did he almost die in a car accident while in college; but before being traded to the Green Bay Packers, after his first season in the league, Favre was diagnosed with a degenerative hip disease which almost stopped the trade.

I THINK FOOTBALL WOULD BECOME
AN EVEN BETTER GAME IF SOMEONE
COULD INVENT A BALL THAT KICKS BACK.

ERIC MORECAMBE

PEYTON MANNING IS THE ONLY PLAYER TO WIN FOUR AP NFL MVP AWARDS. MANNING WON THE AWARD IN 2003, 2004, 2008, AND 2009.

The highest career passer rating is held by Steve Young (96.8). Young could also run the ball, rushing for 43 touchdowns during his illustrious career.

Quite possibly the greatest single college game performance was not accomplished by Peyton Manning or Eli Manning, but rather by their father, Archie Manning. Archie played in the first nationally televised college football game, throwing for 436 yards and 3 touchdowns and running for 104 yards.

A football is made of leather, is approximately eleven inches long and twenty-two inches in circumference at the center, and is slightly pointed at the ends.

Since the NFL Defensive Player of the Year award was first instituted in 1971, several players have won the award twice, but only one player has won the award three times: Lawrence Taylor.

The Heisman trophy is awarded to the most outstanding college football player each year, a designation determined by New York City's Downtown Athletic Club. The trophy, originally called the DAC trophy, was renamed the Heisman trophy in honor of the club's athletic director, John Heisman, after his passing in 1936.

THE RECORD FOR THE HIGHEST PASSER RATING IN A SEASON IS 121.1 SET BY THE COLTS' PEYTON MANNING IN 2004.

Thanks be to God, who gives us the victory through our Lord Jesus Christ.

1 CORINTHIANS 15:57 NRSV

THE OFFICIAL REFEREE SIGNAL FOR A DROPPED PASS, MISSED FIELD GOAL, AND MISSED EXTRA POINT IS THE BASEBALL "SAFE" SIGN.

The Detroit Lions and the Cleveland Browns
are the most storied NFL franchises to never
make an appearance in the Super Bowl.

As far as coaches who coached from 1930 to 2010, none had a higher winning percentage than John Madden, whose .763 win percentage is second all time.

30 ◄**40** **50**

THE BEST SUPER BOWL WIN PERCENTAGE
OF TEAMS APPEARING IN A MINIMUM OF
TWO SUPER BOWLS IS HELD BY THE SAN
FRANCISCO 49ERS WHO ARE 5-0.

Though regarded as too small to succeed in major college football and then the NFL, Emmitt Smith played well enough to be inducted into the College Football Hall of Fame in 2006 and the Pro Football Hall of Fame in 2010.

THE WORDS "DENVER BRONCOS"
AND "JOHN ELWAY" ARE SYNONYMOUS.
ELWAY LED THE TEAM TO BACK-TO-BACK
SUPER BOWL CHAMPIONSHIPS
IN 1997 AND 1998.

THE 1977 TO 1979 DENVER BRONCO DEFENSE WAS DUBBED "THE ORANGE CRUSH," LED BY LINEBACKER TOM JACKSON (LONGTIME ESPN HOST) AND RANDY GRADISHAR.

#1

Troy Aikman was the number one pick of the 1989 NFL draft. He went on to lead the Dallas Cowboys to three Super Bowl victories, winning the Super Bowl MVP in Super Bowl XXVII.

The Pittsburgh Steelers have, hands down, won the most NFL Defensive Player of the Year Awards (6) led by "Mean" Joe Greene who won the award twice.

Five quarterbacks were drafted ahead of Dan Marino in the 1983 NFL draft: John Elway and Jim Kelly were the only two to have distinguished NFL careers.

The NFL Scouting Combine is six days of intense physical and mental testing for potential NFL draft picks. Tests include: the 40-yard dash, bench pressing, a vertical jump, interviews, and drug screening.

THE RECORD FOR MOST PASSING YARDS
IN A SINGLE SEASON WAS SET BY
DAN MARINO IN 1984, WHEN HE
PASSED FOR 5,084 YARDS.

In 2009, Joe Paterno, who holds the record for most Division 1 college football victories, celebrated his sixtieth season as a member of the Penn State Nittany Lions coaching staff.

WITH 8 EACH, ALABAMA AND NOTRE DAME, HAVE WON THE MOST NATIONAL POLL CHAMPIONSHIPS (1936 TO 2009). OKLAHOMA AND USC HAVE EACH WON 7.

The record (if it can be called that) for the most claimed National Collegiate Football Championships (as claimed by schools) is held by Princeton, who claims 28 National Championships dating back to 1869, the last one coming in 1950.

Thanksgiving dinners take eighteen hours to prepare. They are consumed in twelve minutes. Halftimes take twelve minutes.
This is not coincidence.

ERMA BOMBECK

Two states have the most NFL teams: California and Florida each have three. California is home of the Raiders, 49ers, and Chargers. Florida is home of the Dolphins, Buccaneers, and Jaguars.

THE MINIMUM SALARY FOR A
FIRST-YEAR NFL PLAYER IN 2010 IS
$325,000.00. THE MINIMUM SALARY
FOR A PLAYER WITH TEN OR MORE
YEARS EXPERIENCE IS $860,000.00.

Pete Rozelle held the position of NFL commissioner longer than anyone. Rozelle was commissioner from 1960 to 1989. The current commissioner is Roger Goodell.

THE NFL LEAGUE OFFICE IS LOCATED
IN NEW YORK CITY. IT HAS BEEN
LOCATED IN NEW YORK SINCE 1960.

NFL uniform numbers are designated by position in order for fans and referees to more easily identify players. For example, quarterbacks, place kickers, and punters must wear numbers between 1 and 19.

ABC HOSTED *MONDAY NIGHT FOOTBALL* FOR THIRTY-FIVE YEARS FROM 1970 TO 2005. THERE WERE A TOTAL OF 555 MONDAY NIGHT FOOTBALL GAMES AIRED BY ABC.

THE MOST FREQUENTLY AIRED
MONDAY NIGHT FOOTBALL
GAMES HAVE FEATURED DENVER
VS. OAKLAND AND DALLAS
VS. WASHINGTON.

#1

Sports have produced some great nicknames,
but the NFL produced two of the best:
Christian Okoye, "The Nigerian Nightmare"
and Red Grange, "The Galloping Ghost."

The NFL has some great fan nicknames. The Packers fans are known as "Cheeseheads." The Washington Redskins have a group of male fans who wear dresses and pig-noses; they are known as the "Hogettes."

As of 2010, there are 32 teams in the NFL; 16 teams in the AFC; and 16 teams in the NFC. Each conference has 4 divisions (North, South, East, and West) made up of 4 teams in each division.

Don Shula won more games than any other NFL head coach. Shula coached for thirty-three years and won 328 games. As of 2008, no active coach was within a hundred wins of the former Dolphins coach.

The record for most coaching losses is
held by Dan Reeves, who over twenty-three
years lost 165 games. In Reeves' defense,
he also won 190 games for a .535 win percentage.

No coach has won more Super Bowl championships than Chuck Knoll. Knoll won four Super Bowls while coach of the Pittsburgh Steelers in the 1970s.

THE COACH WITH THE HIGHEST WINNING PERCENTAGE ALL-TIME (MINIMUM 80 GAMES COACHED) IS GUY CHAMBERLAIN, WHO WON AN ASTONISHING 78 PERCENT OF THE GAMES HE COACHED FROM 1922 TO 1927.

Notre Dame and USC are the only schools to have seven individuals win the Heisman Trophy. Ohio State has six Heisman trophy winners, but one, Archie Griffin, has won the award twice.

As far as play-off winning percentage is concerned, nobody has bettered Vince Lombardi's winning percentage. Lombardi's teams won 9 of the 10 playoff games he coached.

YOU HAVE TO PLAY THIS
GAME LIKE SOMEBODY JUST
HIT YOUR MOTHER WITH A
TWO-BY-FOUR.

DAN BIRDWELL

The Minnesota Vikings and the Buffalo Bills have appeared in the most Super Bowls without coming up with a win. Both franchises are 0-4 in the Super Bowl.

◄ 10   ◄ 20

BEST NFL DRAFT PICK OF ALL TIME?

Tom Brady, the future Hall of Famer, was the one hundred ninety-ninth overall pick in the 2000 draft. Worst draft pick: hands down, Ryan Leaf, second overall pick in 1998.

30   ◄40   50

Only four safeties have ever won the
NFL Defensive Player of the Year Award:
Ed Reed, Bob Sanders, Dick Anderson,
and Kenny Easley.

The NFL MVP is almost always a quarterback or a running back, but every once in a while another position outshines these two playmaker positions. Lawrence Taylor is the only linebacker to win the award, Mark Moseley the only place-kicker, and Alan Page the only defensive tackle to take the honor.

The official referee signal for a touchdown, extra point, field goal, and two-point conversion is arms raised. A touchdown is worth 6 points, an extra point 1 point, and a field goal 3 points.

The New England Patriots came into existence as the Boston Patriots in 1959. Forty-two years would pass before the team won its first Super Bowl in 2001. They would go on to win the big game two more times in the span of three years.

JOHN ELWAY, OF THE DENVER BRONCOS, WAS SACKED MORE THAN ANY OTHER QUARTERBACK IN HISTORY. ELWAY WAS SACKED 516 TIMES FROM 1983 TO 1998.

The official referee signal for holding (offensive and defensive) is grasping the wrist, fist clenched. Holding results in a 10-yard penalty if it's against the offense; if it's against the defense, it's a 5-yard penalty and an automatic first down.

MORTEN ANDERSON HOLDS THE
RECORD FOR THE MOST GAMES PLAYED.
ANDERSON PLAYED IN 382 GAMES FOR
FIVE DIFFERENT TEAMS OVER A
TWENTY-FIVE-YEAR SPAN.

JERRY RICE, WHO MANY CONSIDER TO BE THE GREATEST WIDE RECEIVER OF ALL-TIME, CAUGHT 1,549 PASSES, 197 RESULTING IN TOUCHDOWNS, DURING HIS CAREER BOTH NFL RECORDS.

30 ◄ 40 50

The official referee signal for an offside call on the defense (crossing the line of scrimmage before the ball is snapped, without being drawn by the offense) is hands to the hips. Results in a 5-yard penalty against the defense.

The Arizona Cardinals are the oldest active team in pro football. Originally called the Morgan Athletic Club, they came into existence in 1899 and have undergone six name changes.

THE NEW ENGLAND PATRIOTS ORIGINAL LOGO WAS THAT OF A PATRIOT, CALLED PAT PATRIOT, SET LIKE A CENTER PREPARING TO SNAP THE FOOTBALL.

The official referee signal for unsportsmanlike conduct is arms stretched out, palms down. Results in a 15-yard penalty and automatic first down if committed by the defense.

OF THE 74 INDIVIDUALS WHO WON THE HEISMAN TROPHY BETWEEN 1935 AND 2009, ONLY 8 HAD BEEN ELECTED TO THE PRO FOOTBALL HALL OF FAME AS OF THE BEGINNING OF 2010.

A TOUCHDOWN IS SCORED WHEN ANY PART OF THE BALL TOUCHES, CROSSES, OR IS ABOVE THE GOAL LINE.

The sideline border is white and six feet wide. Touching it results in out of bounds. In college a receiver must have one foot in bounds when catching a ball; in pro football the player must have both feet in bounds.

*One thing I do: Forgetting what is
behind and straining toward what is
ahead, I press on toward the goal to
win the prize for which God has called
me heavenward in Christ Jesus.*

PHILIPPIANS 3:13–14 NIV

30   ◄ 40   50

GOAL POSTS ARE EIGHTEEN FEET SIX
INCHES WIDE, THE TOP OF THE CROSSBAR
TEN FEET ABOVE THE GROUND, THE
VERTICAL POSTS EXTENDING THIRTY
FEET ABOVE THE CROSS BAR.

A FOOTBALL FIELD IS 360 FEET
LONG, INCLUDING THE (TWO)
30-FEET END ZONES.
THE FIELD IS 160 FEET WIDE.

The coin toss takes place within three minutes of kickoff in the center of the field. The visiting captain calls the toss before the coin is flipped.

If a field goal is attempted beyond the 20-yard line, the defensive team takes possession at the spot of the kick; if a field goal is missed from a spot on or inside the 20-yard line, the defensive team takes possession at the 20-yard line.

30 ◄ 40 50

THE MAXIMUM NUMBER OF PLAYERS ALLOWED ON THE FIELD WHEN THE CLOCK IS RUNNING IS 22, 11 FROM EACH TEAM.

A PRO FOOTBALL GAME IS MADE UP OF (FOUR) FIFTEEN-MINUTE QUARTERS, WITH A TWELVE-MINUTE BREAK AT HALFTIME.

The Pro Football Hall of Fame opened on September 7, 1963, in Canton, Ohio, and included the enshrinement of 17 individuals.

◄10   ◄20

THE OFFICIAL REFEREE SIGNAL
FOR FACEMASK IS ONE HAND,
FIST CLENCHED IN FRONT OF FACE.
RESULTS IN A 15-YARD PENALTY
AND AN AUTOMATIC FIRST DOWN.

As of 2010, the following player numbers have never been enshrined in the Pro Football Hall of Fame: 23, 43, 48, 67, 69, 90, 94, 95, 96, and 97.

Bart Starr, the Hall
of Fame Green Bay Packers
quarterback, was the
two-hundredth pick in
the 1956 draft.

TEXAS HAS PRODUCED MORE
PRO FOOTBALL HALL OF FAMERS
THAN ANY OTHER STATE (27).
PENNSYLVANIA IS SECOND WITH 26.

There have been over fifty football movies made. Five of the best: *Friday Night Lights, Brian's Song, The Blind Side, We Are Marshall,* and *Remember the Titans.*

Many pro football players also had successful acting careers. To name a few: Carl Weathers (Apollo Creed in several of the *Rocky* movies) Merlin Olsen (*Little House on the Prairie*) Jim Brown (many movies and television shows) and Fred Dryer (*Hunter*).

The NFL Stadium with the largest seating capacity (91,704) is FedEx Field in Landover, Maryland, home to the Washington Redskins.

FOOTBALL COMBINES THE TWO WORST THINGS ABOUT AMERICA: IT IS VIOLENCE PUNCTUATED BY COMMITTEE MEETINGS.

GEORGE F. WILL

THE COLLEGE STADIUM WITH THE LARGEST SEATING CAPACITY (107,282) IS BEAVER STADIUM IN STATE COLLEGE, PENNSYLVANIA, HOME TO THE PENN STATE NITTANY LIONS.

30   ‹ 40   50

The NFL Stadium that ranks at the bottom
in seating capacity (61,500) is Soldier Field in
Chicago, Illinois, home to the Chicago Bears.

In order to be considered for the pro football hall of fame, players and coaches must be retired at least five years.

A football helmet is made of hard plastic with thick padding on the inside. Hard plastic bars protect the face, and a chinstrap keeps the helmet in place.

THE SAN DIEGO CHARGERS WERE ORIGINALLY FROM LOS ANGELES. THEY MOVED TO SAN DIEGO IN 1961.

Knute Rockne coached Notre Dame for thirteen years. His winning percentage was just south of 90 percent. He won five national championships before dying in a plane crash at the age of forty-three. President Hoover called his death "a national loss."

There are three types of running backs. Halfbacks and tailbacks primarily run with the football, while it is usually a fullback's job to block for the halfback, tailback, or quarterback.

Tip:

Punting a football: Hold the ball out in front of the body with the right hand on the bottom right side and the left hand on the middle left, making sure the laces are up, ball slightly angled to the left; a right-footed punter then steps forward with the left foot, then the right, again with the left, before kicking with the right.

The Chicago Bears, one of the most storied sports franchises of all-time, has surprisingly only won one Super Bowl. They won the big game in 1985 under the tutelage of Mike Ditka.

#1

Brett Favre played his first NFL season with the Atlanta Falcons. The Falcons coach was not a fan of Favre's. Favre threw 5 passes, completed 0 (well, 2 if you count the interceptions), and was traded to the Green Bay Packers.

Troy Aikman was offered a contract to play baseball for the New York Mets, but chose to play football at the University of Oklahoma. Injured while at OU, he transferred to UCLA where he had two exceptional collegiate seasons.

THE RECORD FOR MOST PASSING YARDS
IN A SINGLE GAME IS HELD BY NORM
VAN BROCKLIN WHO PASSED FOR 554
YARDS ON SEPTEMBER 28, 1951.

THE DALLAS COWBOYS HAVE PARTICIPATED IN THE MOST SUPER BOWLS EVER (8), MEANING THE COWBOYS AVERAGE MAKING IT TO THE BIG GAME ONCE EVERY FIVE TO SIX YEARS.

tip:
Running with the football: Hold the ball in the crook of the arm with the fingers around the nose of the ball.

THE OLDEST BOWL GAME IN COLLEGE FOOTBALL IS THE ROSE BOWL, PLAYED FOR THE FIRST TIME ON JANUARY 1, 1902.

When I went to Catholic high school in Philadelphia, we just had one coach for football and basketball. He took all of us who turned out and had us run through a forest. The ones who ran into the trees were on the football team.

GEORGE RAVELING

Gary Anderson, one of the greatest field goal kickers of all-time, didn't miss a PAT or a field goal during the 1998 season. Unfortunately he missed one in the NFC Championship that season, and his team lost the game.

Only one college offered Brett Favre a scholarship out of high school: Southern Mississippi. The coach wanted him to play defensive back, but Favre wanted to play quarterback. He was initially the seventh-string quarterback.

THE DALLAS COWBOYS HOLD THE RECORD FOR MOST CONSECUTIVE WINNING SEASONS—TWENTY—WHICH THEY ACCOMPLISHED FROM 1966 TO 1985.

Archie Griffin is the only college football player to win the Heisman Trophy twice. Griffin won it back-to-back years while at Ohio State University (1974 and 1975).

THE RECORD FOR MOST FUMBLES IN A SINGLE GAME IS HELD BY LEN DAWSON, WHO FUMBLED THE BALL 7 TIMES ON NOVEMBER 15, 1964.

‹10 ‹20

#1

Kurt Warner, possibly the greatest undrafted player of all time, was invited to try out for the Green Bay Packers, but was released and began stocking shelves at a grocery store for $5.50 an hour. He would later be named the MVP of Super Bowl XXXIV.

Dallas's first team was the Texans. There were actually two Texan teams. The first became the Baltimore Colts, the second the Kansas City Chiefs. The Cowboys came into existence in 1960.

The quarterback receives the ball from the center and can either pass the ball, run with it, or hand it to another player who can either throw it or run with it. On average, a quarterback hands the ball off as often as he throws it. Though some quarterbacks specialize in running with the football, most either pass it or hand it off to a halfback, tailback, or fullback.